Connecticut Fish Species

Game Fish & Panfish

Billy Grinslott & Kinsey Marie Books

ISBN - 9781968228606

Banded Sunfish got their name because they have darker lines that run vertically on their sides. They also have a rounded tail with spots on their body, tail and fins. Banded sunfish are typically only about 2 inches long, making them one of the smallest sunfish. Their small size makes them vulnerable to larger fish, so they thrive in protected areas. Banded sunfish prefer slow-moving, vegetated waters like swamps, ponds, and backwaters of creeks

The Green Sunfish is blue green in color. It has yellow flecks on both its scales and some parts of its sides. The Green Sunfish also has broken blue stripes which is why some people confuse it with the Bluegill. Green Sunfish are very adaptable. They can live in any body of water that has vegetation or weeds. Green sunfish are opportunistic feeders, consuming insects, small fish, and other invertebrates.

The bluegill also considered a sunfish is the most popular fish to fish for. They are called pan fish because they are about the size of a frying pan. Bluegills love to eat insects and bugs. They have good vision and rely on their keen eyesight to feed. Three types in this group are the Bluegill, Sunfish, and Pumpkinseed.

The Warmouth is a member of the Rock Bass, Green Sunfish and Bluegill family. They can survive in low oxygen environments while other fish cannot. Warmouth can thrive in muddy water, when other fish can't. Warmouth are often confused with rock bass. The difference between the two is in the anal fin: warmouth have three spines on the anal fin ray and rock bass have six spines.

The Redbreast sunfish has a red-yellow chest and belly with rusty brown spots on their body. The species is known for its distinctive grunting vocalizations, which are produced by grinding their teeth together. Redbreast sunfish can survive in oxygen-poor environments by using their gills to extract oxygen from air bubbles trapped in aquatic vegetation.

The Pumpkinseed is also known as pond perch, sun perch, and punky's sunfish. It can be found in numerous lakes, ponds, and rivers. It is their body shape resembling the seed of a pumpkin, that inspired their name. Pumpkinseed sunfish have speckles on their orangish colored sides and back, with a yellow to orange belly and chest. They are active during the day and rest at night near the bottom or in shelter areas.

The Atlantic tomcod is a small, bottom-dwelling fish species, also known as a frostfish. They have a slender body, three dorsal fins, two anal fins, a rounded tail. Some people call the Atlantic cod a tomcod, but they are different. While they are related members of the same cod family, they are different species with distinct sizes, habitats, and physical traits, with the tomcod being much smaller and preferring shallow, brackish coastal waters.

White perch grow seven to ten inches in length and rarely weigh more than one pound. They have a silvery body with faint lines on the sides. The white perch is an opportunistic feeder. Young feed primarily on zooplankton and adults feed on aquatic insect larvae, minnows and fish eggs. White Perch is a euryhaline species, inhabiting fresh, brackish and coastal waters. The record for the biggest white perch caught in Connecticut is 3 pounds 1 ounce.

The two most famous perches are the common perch and the yellow perch. The yellow perch has a brilliant greenish yellow color with orange fins. The yellow perch is the biggest one and can grow to a size of 18 inches. It's also known as the jumbo perch. The other type of perch is the white perch. The official Connecticut state record for the biggest yellow perch is a 2-pound, 13-ounce fish

Alewives are anadromous fish that migrate from the ocean to freshwater rivers and streams to spawn. They are small, silvery herring-like fish with a saw-edged belly and a forked tail. Alewives have a distinctive saw-edge on their belly, formed by modified scales called scutes. This feature is used for protection and is also what gives them the nickname saw bellies. While most alewives are anadromous, there are also populations that have become landlocked.

The Rock Bass is not actually a bass but a member of the sunfish family. The biggest Rock Bass ever caught on record weighs about three pounds and was a little over one foot long. Rock bass, like waters with rocky vegetated areas, that's how they got their name. The biggest Rock Bass caught in Connecticut weighed 1 lb. 3 oz.

There are two main types of crappies. The white crappie and the black crappie. They are also members of the sunfish family. The difference between the white and black crappie is one has dark spots and the other has dark lines and is lighter in color. The white crappie has six dorsal fin spines, whereas the black crappie has eight dorsal fin spines. The white crappie can grow bigger and more of the bigger white crappie are caught in North America. The state record for Black Crappie in Connecticut is 4 pounds and 17 inches in length.

The sucker fish has the same mouth as a carp. They got their name because their mouth is like a suction cup. They normally are bottom feeders and suck their food from the bottom of the lake. Many people use sucker fish to fish for northern pike and other big game fish. The White Sucker is a common, large native sucker species, typically reaching 6 to 18 inches long.

The Longnose Sucker is recognized by its long snout, cylindrical body, and thick, papillose lips. They have a dusky gray green to brown back with a white, underside, and a distinctive long snout that overhangs the mouth. Typically, they grow 12 to 18 inches long and live 8 to 20 years. Longnose suckers are bottom feeders that use their fleshy lips to vacuum up algae, midge larvae, small mollusks, and various aquatic invertebrates.

The black, brown and yellow bullhead are part of the catfish family. They usually only grow to about 10 inches long. They use their whiskers to help find food. The bullhead is the most common member of the catfish family. Bullheads live in the water containing low oxygen levels. They can survive on low oxygen areas, where other fish can't. The record for the largest brown bullhead (hornpout) caught in Connecticut is a 5.45-pound fish.

The Channel Catfish are the most fished catfish species with around 8 million anglers fishing for them per year. Channel catfish have taste buds all over their body, making them highly sensitive to the taste and smell of food. They also have barbels (whiskers) around their mouths, which are used for sensing and tasting food. They use sound waves to communicate with each other. They can also produce alarm substances to warn other catfish of danger. The official Connecticut state record for the biggest Channel Catfish caught is 29.4 pounds.

The madtom is a small catfish that is native to the eastern United States. Madtoms are scaleless fishes with eight whisker-like barbels around their mouths used as sensors. The madtom feeds on the bottom at night, using its sensitive barbels, whiskers to touch and taste for food. Its diet consists mostly of aquatic insects.

White catfish are interesting because they are smaller than other common catfish species like channel catfish, they have a wider head and lack the black spots of channel catfish. White catfish are the smallest of the large North American catfish species. The White catfish has white chin barbells, which distinguish it from other species. There are four pairs of barbels, whiskers around the mouth, two on the chin, one at the angle of the mouth, and one behind the nostril. The biggest white catfish caught in Connecticut weighed 21.3-pounds.

Bowfins can breathe both air and water, putting them at an advantage in low-oxygen waters. Bowfins are often described as prehistoric relics. This is because species can be traced to fossils from the Cretaceous, Eocene and Jurassic period. The largest Bowfin (Amia calva) on record in Connecticut weighed 9 pounds.

Striped bass are often called Stripers. Striped bass live in both salt and fresh water. Striped bass have very sensitive eyes and will seek deep water when the sun is out. Striped bass have a preferred water temperature range of from 55° F to 68° F, and swim to find water of these temperatures. White Bass are related to Striped Bass and have lighter stripes on their sides. The biggest striped bass caught in Connecticut weighed 81 lbs. 14oz.

The burbot, also known as the eel pout. They get their name because they have a serpent-like or eel-like body. They can wrap their tail around things. There's nothing to worry about if you catch one, they may try to wrap their tail around your arm, but they are harmless. Burbots are adapted to cold water and are found in large, cold rivers, lakes, and reservoirs, primarily preferring freshwater habitats. Burbots are also known as ling, cusk, or eelpout.

Sturgeons have sharp spines on their back, so be careful when handling them. Instead of scales, sturgeon skin is covered in bony plates called scutes, which can be very sharp on young sturgeon. Sturgeons have been around since the dinosaur days. Sturgeons mostly live in large, freshwater lakes and rivers. Their average lifespan is 50 to 60 years. One of the largest sturgeons recorded in the Connecticut River was a specimen weighing over 260 pounds.

Carp have long been an important food fish to humans. Carp are bottom feeders for the most part and their mouth is made like a suction cup, so they can suck food off the bottom. Carp are good for a lake because they help clean the bottom of the lake. The biggest carp caught in Connecticut is a 58.05-pound (44.8-inch) common carp.

The rainbow trout gets its name because of its brilliant colors. Rainbow trout populations are good indicators of water pollution because they can only survive in clean waters. They like to live in rivers and streams. Rainbow trout rank among the top five most sought game fish in North America. The record for the largest rainbow trout caught in Connecticut is a 15 lb. 12 oz. fish.

The lake trout is one of the biggest of the trout family. The biggest lake trout caught was 72 pounds. Lake trout like to live in lakes that are deep. They like being in the cool water in the deep parts of a lake. They have been reported to live up to 70 years in some Canadian lakes. The biggest lake trout caught in Connecticut weighed 29 pounds, 13 ounces.

Brook trout are characterized by their olive-green bodies with pale, worm-like markings, red spots with bluish halos, and orange-red fins with white and black edges. They can grow up to 12 inches in length. Brook trout are cold-water fish that prefer clean, clear, and cold streams, lakes, and ponds. The biggest Brook trout caught in Connecticut is 9.2 pounds and 28 inches long.

Brown trout can live up to 20 years. Brown trout have a higher tolerance for warmer waters than either brook or rainbow trout. Brown trout can be found on almost every continent except Antarctica, and many can be found living in the ocean. They have olive-brown, yellow-orange, or silvery sides with a mix of black, red, and orange spots. The largest Brown trout caught in Connecticut weighed 19 lbs.

Tiger trout are known for their aggressive nature and awesome looking tiger-like stripes. Tiger trout are not naturally occurring in the wild, but rather a hybrid created by mixing a female brown trout with a male brook trout. They are stocked in lakes and rivers. Their striking appearance with tiger-like stripes and patterns, makes them easily recognizable. They are known to grow faster than their parent species. The largest Tiger trout caught in Connecticut is a 7-pound, 14-ounce fish.

The primary salmon species you'll find are landlocked sockeye salmon, also known as kokanee. These are the non-anadromous form of sockeye salmon, meaning they don't migrate to the ocean. They live their entire lives in freshwater lakes and reservoirs. The biggest Kokanee salmon caught in Connecticut weighed 2 lbs. 14 oz and measured 21 inches.

Atlantic salmon are anadromous, meaning they live in both freshwater and saltwater. Atlantic Salmon are present in Connecticut, primarily as landlocked fish in inland lakes and tributaries rather than sea-run fish. They are known for their impressive leaping abilities, allowing them to jump over waterfalls and obstacles to reach spawning grounds. Atlantic salmon change color when they return to freshwater to spawn, becoming a rusty-bronze color with red markings.

The largemouth bass is the most sought-after bass in North America. Largemouth bass live in just about every lake in North America. They have great hearing and can hear a crayfish crawling on the bottom of the lake. Connecticut's state record largemouth bass is a massive 12 pounds, 14 ounces.

Smallmouth bass have a smaller mouth than the largemouth bass. They also have different markings and are lighter in color. They don't live in most lakes because they prefer living in colder water. They are typically found in the northern states in America because the water is cooler. The current world record smallmouth is an 11-pound, 15-ounce fish. They can be found in lakes, reservoirs, and rivers. The official Connecticut state record for Smallmouth bass is a 7-pound, 12-ounce fish.

The walleye got its name because of its white looking eyes. Their eyes collect light, even in low light conditions. This means they can see in the dark. Because they can see in the dark, they mostly feed at night. During the daytime their eyes are very sensitive, so they usually head for deeper water or shady places. Walleye like to live in cooler water and are normally found in the upper part of North America. The biggest walleye caught in Connecticut is a 15.23-pound (or 15 lbs. 4 oz) record-setting fish.

Pickerel kind of look like northern pike, but they are not. The Pike is larger in size than the Pickerel. The Pickerel has more spots than the Pike, but the Pike has spots on its fins and pickerel don't. Pickerel has a dark bar beneath their eyes and northern pike don't. Pickerel are also known as gunfish or slime darts. The record for the largest Chain Pickerel caught in Connecticut is 8.6 pounds

The Redfin Pickerel is a small, solitary freshwater fish in the pike family, typically measuring 10–15 inches and living 8–10 years. They inhabit clear, slow-moving, heavily vegetated streams and swamps. They are ambush predators feeding on small fish, crustaceans, and insects. They are olive to yellowish green with distinct, bright red-orange fins and a dark, backwards-slanting bar beneath the eye.

The Northern Pike is one of the most sought-after fish for anglers. It got its name because it likes to live in cooler water mainly in the northern states of North America. The northern pike is a very aggressive predator. They don't like to live in groups with other fish, they are very territorial and like to live alone. Their behavior is closely affected by weather conditions. The biggest Northern Pike caught in Connecticut is a 29-pound fish measuring 46 inches long.

Another breed of the Muskie is the tiger muskie. The tiger muskie is a cross between the northern pike and muskie. They grow larger and faster than normal muskies and northern pikes. The tiger muskie got its name because it has tiger like stripes. Tiger Muskies are very rare and hard to catch. The world record tiger muskie is a massive fish weighing 51 pounds, 3 ounces. The biggest tiger muskie reported in Connecticut is a 42-inch fish, weighing over 26 pounds.

Fun Facts About Connecticut Fish

1 - The American shad (Alosa sapidissima) is the official state fish of Connecticut, designated in 2003.

2 - Unlike other salmon, the brook trout lack teeth on the roof of their mouth. They rely on their bottom teeth to grab food.

3 - The lake sturgeon is the granddaddy of all fish. They can live up to 100 years and weigh up to 300 pounds.

4 - The largest freshwater fish ever recorded in Connecticut is a 58.05-pound, 44.8-inch common carp.

5 - Key game fish include largemouth/smallmouth bass, walleye, northern pike, and various trout (brook, brown, rainbow).

6 - The burbot, also known as eelpout, is a member of the freshwater cod family and has an odd habit of wrapping its slimy tail around the hand or arm of anglers.

7 – Notable record-sized fish include. Largemouth Bass: 12 lb. 11 oz. Channel Catfish: 29 lb. 6 oz. Lake Trout: 29 lb. 13 oz. Northern Pike: 29 lb.

Author Page

Billy Grinslott & Kinsey Marie Books

ISBN – 9781968228606

Thanks

www.ingramcontent.com/pod-product-compliance
Lightning Source LLC
Chambersburg PA
CBHW060850270326
41934CB00002B/68